Contents

Crazy Weather: The Facts

Tornadoes

A tornado is a column of air spinning very fast.

When hot air meets cold, dry air high up, it starts spinning. Air from the ground is sucked up.

Tornadoes can smash buildin
and pull up trees.

Hurricanes

Hurricanes are very bad storms.

They start over the sea. When they move inland, they cause really bad damage.

Flooding after a hurricane.

Thunder and lightning

Tiny pieces of ice in clouds move around and bump into each other. This makes electricity build up.

This electricity flashes to the ground. This is lightning.

When it happens there is a huge bang. This is thunder.

Lightning can cause serious damage.

Blizzards and ice storms

Heavy snow storms with strong wind are called blizzards.

Blizzards make life very difficult.

Ice storms are caused
by freezing rain.

They can do a lot of damage.

Floods

Heavy rain may cause floods.
Rivers can overflow.

Floods can cause serious damage.

Drought

Droughts happen when there isn't enough rain!

Some rivers and lakes dry up.

Plants and animals may die.

NO

SWIMMING

The land can turn into a desert where no one can live.

Things that fall from the sky

Sometimes it rains
more than just rain ...

Fish (in the desert!)

Blood

Frogs

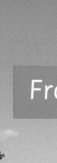

Fresh meat

100s of dead birds

We think storms pull these things into the air ...

... and then they fall to the ground.

Breaking the world record

Hottest: Lut desert, Iran. 71°C.

Wettest: Sohra, India. 1,000 inches of rain a year.

Coldest: Ridge A, Antarctica. Minus 70°C.

Windiest: Commonwealth Bay, Antarctica. 200 mph.

Is the climate changing?

Yes.

Why is it happening?

Is it our fault?

The Flood

Look out, Rob!

The car hits a bridge ...

They're safe – but only just!

34

Mum and Dad are safe, too ...

Word list

blizzard
bridge
climate
column
crazy
damage
drought
electricity

flood
hurricane
lightning
serious
thunder
tornado
weather